Copyright © 2021

Hermione (Mona) Rimson-Hope

All rights reserved. No part of this publication may be reproduced, stored in a retrieval system or transmitted in any form or by any means – electronic, mechanical, photocopying, and recording or otherwise – without the prior written permission of the author. To perform any of the above is an infringement of copyright law.

Contents

Chapter one: Women Empowering   Page 5

Chapter two: For real   Page 25

Chapter three: Still Standing   Page 55

Chapter four: Logic   Page 71

Chapter five: Questions & Answers   Page 85

Acknowledgments

My reason for what I do. To my best friend my mom (Mattie Pruitt) my little girl still 99 years strong. Her wisdom and strength are my motivation. Fourth shot at putting my wisdom and emotional senses of being on paper. As I continue to explore what I've learn from you this life. "Damn I'm even more excited."
Always believe in you because you can never go wrong. Even if someone tries to tell you it isn't so. Accept where you are right now in life and acknowledge your feelings.

Introduction

Soothing the soul- being in the element of your thoughts. Knowing what we've learn can sooth the soul. Keeping a journal of your thought and experiences will help you appreciate yourself more. Knowing you are helping yourself enjoy life from every element. Be mindful of what you think and what you display. During this new normal.

Chapter 1

Women Empowering

Best Friend

Love yourself be your own best friend. We must love ourselves first. You can't love anyone else until you love you. You are the one person that you'll never get rid of. Every move you make you make with you. Spend time reviewing yourself to see why you don't like yourself. God so love you he forgave his only begotten son. Hug yourself.

Chronicles

There is no instruction manual on birth till death. It's played out day by day. We have a lot of instructor's parents, pastors, mentors, counselors, friends and enemies. Stop fretting over the story line and the ending. Live comfortably without all the details because your destiny is already determined by God. Be at peace with yourself from within beginning to the end.

Distinction

We are distinctive in how we nurture, care, encouraging growth and the development of others. Especially our children and others we encounter. As we define from within. When I leave this place I want to leave my fingerprints on someone.

Distractions

Don't mess up a friendship on distractions. Everything being presented is the representative. Look at what you know. Don't become a statistic with no benefits.

Dollar Bill

You can be anybodies best friend for a price. But when you're not loyal or valued they won't? Fill in the blank

Facade

There is nothing stronger than a woman who has rebirth herself. When she's broken her soul rejuvenates her. Her scars are her lessons. She doesn't let her pass define her. Her loyalty is her love. We're fragile we love hard and we are the best at what we do. It's a journey one that's unique and vintage.

High Standards

Find you a friend not a frenemy who can ignore your flawed fence and admire your flowered garden.

Mean Black Women

We beg for the world and society to see us as we are. But among ourselves we hate on each other. We don't support each other through our ruff times are dysfunctional relationships. Why because we let our own fears of what's hidden in our closets afraid it may come to light. Our actions speak louder than words. We say we love you to each other and it's over used to mask our true feelings and inter being.

Meanie

Being mean isn't an accident it's intentional. What do you expect in return? If someone is mean to you. You get offended. So practice what you preach. Do unto others as you would have them do unto you. Stop being mean. It doesn't pay in the long run.

Black Table Talk

1. What defines us as Women?
2. How she speaks.
3. What Life's destiny she seeks.
4. How she sees herself.
5. Create a mailbox of things for God to do.
6. What she says to identify herself.
7. I appreciate me.

Reflect

Women who go from man to man never finding that man for having daddy issues. Daddy's gone. Why does someone have to tell you the value of what's in your temple.
"It's Your Body"

Rule of Life

You don't want your kids to grow up like you did. Every parent should want their kids to have a better life. That's rule number one of parenting. It doesn't change who you are are what you believe. You're not bougie. You are a great person and a great parent. Protect your kids.

Smothering

Your children have wings that work. Being over protective and over bearing is not going to stop them. We must stop and let them teach themselves. They will fall down. You can't always help them back up. Step back

Straight Talk

You can lose yourself in a relationship just pleasing the other person. Because eventually you are going to miss you somewhere in the relationship. Regrets will form. And you're going to ask what happen to me. Spend time by yourself each person is responsible for their own happiness and fulfillment.

Three (3) characters

1. The long haul friendship the confidant who loves you unconditionally. They are into you and every aspect of your life.

2. The constituents they are not into you. They are into what you are for as long as you on the same page as they are. They will be there for the benefit rewards.

3. The comrades they are not for you are anything you're trying to do. They hang around because whatever you're against they are against. The frenemy are enemy. Messy they will not help you achieve your dreams.

Look at your friends, frenemies and enemies and ask them if they are happy for you.

Tears

My finger tips are like windshield wipers they wipe the tears away. But the pain still remains. The tears come when you're sad are someone breaks your heart. Are when you're filled with joy. Tears are an expression of what your heart can't say.

Transpose

Those that appear as devils in your life
Ask God to expose their devil spirits in
the form of Angels.

Secret to Empowerment in Women

1. Provide the ticket to a better life.
2. Support women and girls in crisis.
3. Mentor a girl close to home.
4. Invest in a small business owner.
5. Use your voice to help keep girls in school.
6. Help a new mom.
7. Tell the women in your life that you care.
8. Be genuine in your purpose.
9. Never forget where you come from.
10. No that you're never alone.

'Soldiers'

God puts his toughest battles on his strongest soldiers'. Hold me up I'm one of his soldiers.

Chapter 2

Age of Altitudes

The difference between salt and sugar hardly none.

The difference between a grin and a smile hardly none.

The difference between looking back and what's behind you hardly none.

The difference between having a plan and a dream hardly none.

The difference between having what you want and not having it is you.

There is no reason it can't come to pass it's you.

Assignment

We are here on an assignment. So when your time expires have you concluded your assignment? Do you know what your assignment was or is? Have you paid attention? What legacy will you leave? Where have your foot prints been left in the sand? Has your voice been heard? There are so many questions with no definitive answers. Check your assignments in your daily routine. So you can say job well done.

A Quilt

In our lives the places we go the roads we travel. The relationships we go through and the triumphs. The people who make a difference, the hurts. The smiles and tears we cry. These are patches that come together as a road map of what has been. How many patches do you have to make your quilt?

It will cover you and keep you warm

Breathe

Drop it, leave it, let it go,
Change the channel
Unsubscribe
Un-friend
Un-follow
Mute
Block
God will fight your battle.

Call Him

If you're waiting on a break through without a battle Pay attention God only calls if he needs you. If he doesn't he'll still keep you. All battles don't turn into wars.

Compartmentalize

Divide into sections to temporarily respite from mental stress. Learn to create mental partitions in your life. It helps to prevent emotional overload.

Definitely

We have always misrepresented God in crisis. We want to blame him for matters of truth. Whatever may be going on at that time that we don't understand. Is it Gods fault are man's fault? The pandemic we're going through?

Is the crisis waking us up? Why we sleep walk and argue. The same attitudes the same discrimination and behaviors are going on.

God doesn't discriminate, argue, are have an attitude. So stop blaming God for mans actions. Look at the one who is. He's a man.

Dreams

Dreams are a collection of our subconscious and conscious thoughts that are managed in our everyday life. Dreams tell you what you really know and about what you really feel. They point you toward what you need for growth, integration, expression, and the health of your relationships with people, place and thing. They can help fine-tune you towards your unfinished business. They're reality machines. And they never lie.

They are suppressed thoughts that have been there throughout our lives. That's why we can control our actions.

Feelings

The feelings you feel are temporary. When you're sad it goes away. When you're happy it goes away. When you grieve it gets better with time. When you love someone it goes away and when you're hurt. Feelings are desires of the mind not the heart. Do well in good times and cherish what you're experienced good or bad. This too shall pass.

Find Me

Some people don't read the Bible. God wrote the words a long time ago. But what was written then is coming to pass now. Pick up the Bible so you will know where you are.

Foundation

Your feet are your foundation. In order for you to stand, walk, climb, step or raise your leg. They are the main support no matter how tall, are short your birth flaws are. You need them. Imagine no feet.

Think of a way to leave your foot prints in the sand.

Growth Wounds

In your journey you will collect scars. Some big some small, yet the destiny to get to your destiny the scrapes and scars are worth it. They will get smaller but those scars will never fade. You will only get stronger.

Heart Song

The difference in each heart in side of us is. Every heart has a legacy. Every heart beats differently. Every heart loves differently. Every heart hurts differently. But each heart that beats one day will stop. The beauty of your heart is what your legacy was.

Hood Life

The best soul food is cooked in the hood.

Best friends you ever had are from the hood.

Best life lessons were learned in the hood.

The best Baptist churches are in the hood.

Best life chapters are taken with you when you leave the hood.

Impact to Murder

We live in a culture of victim blaming. That's call manipulation. Any kind of

abuse is a disease. Placing blame doesn't solve the issues are lessen the incident. Both parties need to be aware.

Inner Fear

You only fear what you can remember that scared you.

Man

M – Manly

A – Awesome

N – Needed

Needs VS. Wants

Don't mistake needs for wants. What you want is attention, money, car, house, freedom, friend and family. What I need is God, trust, respect, food, water, clothing, shelter, air and companionship. Needs are essential for survival. Wants they make life a little more enjoyable.

Don't let your needs turn into wants.

One on One conversation

Everything you do is like attending school. Not just in a classroom do you have to learn. It can be in your walk with everyday life. Focus! There is something for you to learn all the time. Try and take something away with every interaction and conversation. Take something away to teach, empower and guide you. Please

Peace at last

When things don't bother you like they use too it's called a Peace of Mind.

Purgatory God Rules

We are the battle between God and the Devil. That is why our lives are being pulled apart. This life is purgatory. This is where we try to cleanse our souls. Some will go to heaven and some won't. Between good, bad, hate and killing of each other. Reflecting on the Devil he wants to rule in our lives. Those that are weak are influenced. Those that read the Bible and try to live right also struggle. As long as we fall prey to the Devil we will struggle. There is no unity, no trust, no love and no assurance. Our lives are being lived out by the scriptures written in the Bible. Pick up your Bible because God was our creator and ruler.

Refocusing

When we let positive energy in we create a new beginning and understanding to go forward. Past negative thoughts can relapse sounding like a broken record. If we can be mindful of the moment without getting reattached. We can learn to breathe and find self-compassion with ourselves. Let positive thoughts be the new default mode.

See Me

How you look how you speak, present yourself and open doors. Remember is your representative. Stop being fake look the part it's your audition.

Secret and Lies

The book of Luke chapter 12; verse 2

There is nothing covered, that shall not be revealed neither hidden that shall not be known.

Check your skeletons in your closet. They can reveal your true identity.

This Life

If you were born you will die. It's the life you're given that should be lived to the fullest. Enjoy life day by day sharing a smile, a laugh and happiness. Not hate, envy or jealousy. It's ok to be sad and experience panic, but no one should die early. Remember just don't let sadness and madness rule your life.

Valued

If you don't see the value in yourself.
Then stop trying to convince me.

Woman

W – Wise

O – Outstanding

M – Mothers

A – Awesome

N - Nice

Words

If you keep drinking water from the wrong well, you will always be thirsty. Renew yourself by drinking God's word you will never be thirsty again.

Your purpose

Life is filled with criticism and critics. People will talk but it doesn't mean they know what they're talking about. Don't get distracted talk is cheap.

Chapter 3

Author & Finisher

We review our lives as chapters and seasons. Sometimes when trouble comes we look at this as the end of a life. Some things we can fix some things we can't. It's not the whole story are the end.

A mission statement

Walk into a room to motivate, inspire, uplift and support. Helping people to be greater within them self. Inspiring them to be a greater version of them self.

Clash

To know me is to like me.

To experience me is to learn me. To study me is to wonder what I'm about. Find your own enter being. By learning, experiencing, studying and teaching. Be whole mediate learn who you are before trying to learn someone else.

I Talk To Me

People Who Talk to Themselves Aren't Crazy, They're Actually Geniuses

Jesus Jesus Jesus

Conversations

Conduct

Character

Learn who Jesus is

Just As I am

Fierce, loyal, loving, genuine, giving, caring, sharing, wonderer, teaching, learning, inspirer, prayer. motivator and hopefully waiting to explore every element of me. What more can I say.

About me

My Prayer

God I don't understand. I have no idea what's going on. Help me to learn to pray the right way for the right things. I do believe. I may never understand but I will try. I hurt, I laugh and I pray. Forgive me for me. My battles are yours, my vision is yours. I know you're not focused on my faults are flaws. I will stay in faith your will be done. Amen

Moments of Truth

Turn back moments we all have them. If you give up on your dreams because you don't get the support you need.

Because that break didn't come. That doesn't mean that day will never come. Strong belief starts with you. Keep trying, dream big and believe in you. There is a moment you can go forward are you can give up. Faith will sustain you through. So why turn back.

Prescription

Look at what you do for yourself as your medicine. Most people hate how you do you and what you may do for others. Be true to yourself never sharing your medicine. It was prescribed only for you.

Seeds

A Seeds that's US it has to be planted in dirt. Has to have dirt for growth and development. Dirt builds character. When people throw dirt on you it should help strengthen you and share in the development of your core. It's that push through factor soil that helps your seed to sprout and grow. "That's you"

Step into the Light

God is showing you when to step into a meltdown. So as not to offend or be over bearing. When you're dealing with you, you and you. Called those multiple personalities that we all have. Each one requires a different answer to accomplish that task. Attempting to resolve whatever may be occupying that space in between your ears called a mind. Talking to your self is great therapy. You're not crazy just complex.

Who Me

How dare you try and judge me. You only see what I choose to let you see.

Why Argue

My purpose is to impact people. I don't care if you like me. Opinions mean nothing unless you have all the facts.

Unbreakable

Who are you to judge me because my life it's as yours. My relationship it's as yours. My goals and aspirations aren't as yours. But my life is good it's in a good space. I have achieved some of my goals. My aspirations come daily. Can you say the same thing?? Not really because you have to constantly remind yourself. Does judging someone else causes you to remind yourself of what you think you have?

Ask Me Your Questions!

Chapter 4

Logic

A Haters Heart

Haters fix your heart

Make sure its Gods thread you use to fix your broken heart.

Astral body

The enemy is the accuser. Stay relaxed in your Soul. Ask, believe and receive.

Balance

Life is a mystery. You will not know what's in store if you remove the mystery. If the mystery is gone then you won't need Faith. Faith works best when you don't know. We are put in uncompromising situations to unbalance us. Not depending on what we know should make us go deeper inside ourselves it helps build core.

Backwards

If you keep going backwards looking for the person are persons whom you need to walk away from. You will not have room for what God has for your life ahead.

Bible Study

Read a scripture

Study the word

Repeat the word
Acknowledge God

Pray for forgiveness

Prepare yourself

Understand the scripture and follow what is taught. Believe what you've read. Live by Faith. Most importantly understand it all.

Counterfeiter

There is only one narrow pathway to peace. If you're looking for Peace in lustful thoughts and material possessions. All those things create chaos in your heart. Peace is fragile. Holding anger and animosity makes things worse. You can't have peace being trapped in yourself. Find that pathway to peace for you to develop a relationship with God.

Emotional connect

Every emotion is connected by feelings, talking, touching and crying etc. We all have pain and flaws. How we connect with each other determines the outcome of our relationships. To cry doesn't make us weak. Tears are like the rain it makes us stronger. Admitting your strength and weakness makes you a better person. Acknowledge Try it

Flawless

Can you learn without contradicting yourself? Holding conversations with one self are ok. Think about the balance and harmony you maintain when you ask and answer yourself. No harm done and none intended.

Food for thought

People always have you working on your weakness. Focus on your goals. Whatever set your goals as your vision your goals are your strength. Write down your goals and plant them in your subconscious so it will sprout.

Grief

Measure of your lost is the measure of a blessing.

Everyone lives on in some way or some fashion. Enable yourself you are the strength to win from within. There is no time limit on grief.

Heart Breaks

If you let your heart break and the more it breaks. The bigger and stronger your heart becomes. That's how it builds its capacity to Love.

Humble

Every grave is six (6) feet deep. Every urn holds ashes. It shouldn't matter how big your house is or your bank account. Respect everyone and don't forget where you come from. You were born with nothing. Everything is earned.

Hush Up

Your tongue can not be trusted when your heart is filled with vengeance. Hush be quiet until you heal.

Chapter 5

Questions & Answers

Awaken to Life

Poor judgment

Fear

self doubt

there's a spiritual connection.

They're all connected threw you trusting yourself. Go within you to find that trust factor. Intimacy is not something always shared with others. It can be shared with you yourself. Go deep and find a cozy atmosphere or place to get acquainted with you. That peaceful place.

Les Gens =(People)

We as a people have the right to be angry. Whatever emotion you feel you have the right to feel. Knowing how to generate that angry is a life long struggle and learning process. There's good angrier and there's bad angrier based on your spirit's interpretation. Our emotions are all over the place at times. You never know what you're getting. Think about what we need in order to keep the balance. The way we were nurtured is what we give our kids, our friends and our relationships with others. Be proud of who you are and choose wisely on what you will be come.

My Leadership

We all want to be leaders. Make all the decisions. We get offended when others try and guide us. We all are looking for hope and faith to support us. The best thing you can do is turn leadership over to God. His plan has everything for life.

Logic

Part of your mental space is to take time to observe what someone is saying to you. Stop take time to put logic with what you've heard. Go into that shrink mode. From within find that safety space. Pay attention.

Lots

We should review our relationships with others as lots. Most of them are large spaces consuming time. Like different cars and different objects. Point is the people in your lives need to be sorted by their differences and rolls they play in your life. So in order for things to change in your life you have to change the people you lot with.

Never give up

We have a tendency to put more into others than ourselves looking for our roll. We stop pursuing us because we lose the drive and motivation. Always looking back on regrets that we shouldn't have. Always helping others and giving up on ourselves. Stop Self-preservation comes first. Look inside what do hear and see? Un-fog your mirror so you can see your reflection.

Push

God gives you signs when it's time to make a change. Sometimes we don't jump. Then God wines up pushing you. He creates situations to make you take a look. In your job, relationships are any life circumstances. Most times we ignore our life calling. Doing work we don't enjoy. Don't let fear keep you from you.

"The Bible says your Gift will make room for you and put you in the presence of great men."

Punches

Hey sometimes we take psychological punches from someone. Don't take it personal. They are hurting and desperately trying to seek help. Recognize that you need to listen because it's not your turn yet. That is to be understood. Asking for help through punches it's always a fight.

Power Up

You're blessed everyday to wake up. So you need to power up and give thanks for another day. Gear your mind in the right direction. Say you're going to have a good day, a prosperous day, a day full of grace and praise. Receive Gods strength as your power aid.

P.P.P.

Pain

Passion

Purpose

Pain it hurts its how you deal and survive it.

Passion your desire for something new it's how it makes you feel.

Purpose the end result of how your pain and passion fulfilled you to reach your purpose in life.

Roots

Seasonal people get mixed up with life expectations. Some only give shade. Some are like branches. Choose the root they are strong and will last.

Safety

Safety is an internal emotion. We are the only ones that can make us safe. It happens when we lose control and start letting go of those things we fear. A broken relationship
Lost of Love
Death of a love one
Lost of a job
Failure at its best that triggers us to go into Safety Mode.

Set it Off

Turn up on T. D. Jakes, Joel Osteen, Paula White, Joyce Meyers, Creflo Dollar and Steven Fortick. Stop tuning up on what you think is best to hear. When you should be listening to the true word being spoken?

Self Crush

You never post an ugly picture of yourself on Tweeter, Facebook, Instagram or Snap chat. What you post is only your illusion of how you see yourself. It's not how others see you.

Septic

Negative thoughts come into your mind. Sometimes they fester causing unwanted thoughts and feelings. Fight back Believe in fighting your fears, doubt and poor judgment.

Shields

The armor of God is spiritual. He's not on board with the guns, bullet proof vest and lies. There is armor for your heart called faith, hope and love. If you walk with Gods armor the Devil will not get through. He will try and make you doubt yourself. But wear your armor. He cannot win. Those that are liars belong to the devil. Those that are believers belong to God. Choose your armor wisely.

Stair Case

In front of you there are 20 stairs. You say oh my I can't climb those stairs. If you are a goal seeker with a destiny just focuses on the next steps the ones you'll need to reach the top.

Trust and Believe

You're only going to get out of life what you put into it. There are examples:

You give love you receive love.

You display hate you get hate in return.

You plant an apple tree you get an apple.

You give respect you get respect.

You promise to worship God your rewards will come.

You have Faith you can conquer anything.

Voices

Often times we listen to what other people have to say about us. We focus unknowingly on the negative. Becoming caught up in anxiety and disbelief about who we are. Voices back and forth in your head doubt resurfacing. Remember the enemy is the accuser. I can't hear you

Walk with Me

If you walk with pigeons. You'll enjoy learning to fly with eagles. Examine your acquaintances.

Are you God???

You have to be careful about other people's opinions. It's what you ask for that causes opinions to cause pain. How you perceive yourself doesn't require an opinion. Was I God??

Only a Word

When you speak on it until you see it. Finding that word to ground you and teach you. When you're weak and worn-out God will place things in your life to build you up and bless you up. No weapon formed against you will prosper. Don't come to a battle and try to win the war without positive words.

Begin with the End

Where are you in your story? Who can you trust to take the pen from your hand and bring your story to completion? What do you want to be when you grow up? The answer changes like the wind. You never truly grow up enough to know who are are what you will become. Open your mind your eyes so you may see. "You"

Blank

When you know too much you stop living your best self. Staying in one place you won't grow. Being OK with you is essential. Grow but don't. Fill in the blank

Can you hear Me?

Are you alright? After you've done all that you can do? Will you be honest in your answer? There are three questions that should be thought and answered truthfully. There is only one person who will care and who will be receptive of your response. Stop telling others your business they honestly don't care. Why? Because they have their own questions that need answers. Hope they are straight up and honest with the only person who is truly listening. Can you hear me, can you hear me now?

Cynicism and Hope

Why do we think everything has to be our way? Why do we think the worst in everything? Why is it we don't trust anyone? Why are we divided? Hope is the essence of things seen and not yet seen. There is Hope if we learn we are different. We can disagree, yet try and believe.

Double Minded

A double minded person is battling with what they want to be and who they want to become. That's why they oppose what God is saying and trying to show them. They think they're smarter than God. "Really"
He sees all and knows all.

Elevator Music

You rise above the 100th floor. The whole time you're going up what are you really thinking about? What are you really feeling? Do you hear any music or any other sounds? Do you realize the higher up you go the closer to God you are. I rise up in spite of all that is going on in my life.

Fight

People! Do you know what it's like to be on a rock by yourself trying to fight things that are attempting to pluck Faith out of your mind - Hope out of your Spirit - Vision out of your heart? God is teaching you that HE is the friend who sticks closer than a brother or sister! This is how you learn to worship & lean on Him!

He, She and I

In most conversations most people speak in third person. Speaking of themselves as He, She, They or I. Did you answer your question?

Did you solve your problem?

Hoarder

Are you an emotional hoarder? Holding your hurt, anxiety, resentment, and grudges? Cluttering your mind it's not visible to others. They can't see your mind. It's the negative emotions that can be detrimental. They may cause you to lose your temper and having disagreements with others. You must find a way to let go. Since it already happened it's not good to keep holding and reliving. Find a way from within to let go.

Image One

We get all screwed up in our life quest.
Because it's the pictures in our head of
how life is suppose to be?

Intense Fellowship

When you argue are you aware of what you're arguing about? It is about control and running the show. Can we agree to disagree?

Yes we can!!!!

An argument sometimes leads to resentment. Because when negative feelings surface communication is gone.

Communication is the key to keeping it together. Don't go to bed mad at each other.

Letter to heaven

Have you ever thought about writing a letter to Heaven?

Just think about all the things you could talk about?

Birth, death, love, hate, life, peace, war, racism, discrimination, mental health, disabilities, anger, happiness, resentment, disease and cancer it goes on and on.

What would you be asking Heaven to do?

Think, Ask Write

Love Is

Love is an action not just a theory are words. It's received better when you can feel it. Do you feel what I'm trying to tell you? You can read it and theorize you can say it and never mean it. But your actions when you do it are better understood and received. Ask yourself what is love to me?

Mediocrity

How do see yourself
Average, ordinary successful? In all
areas of life we look at ourselves in some
way as great, better, smarter are just
like whatever. Being exceptional elevates
everyone it touches. Mediocrity is telling
so as to never have fear of failure or low
expectations for yourself. Always reach
beyond your current performance to be
exceptional at being you.

Mine Eyes

Seeing things my eyes their weak. My vision has changed. My thoughts are obscured, my heart is pure. But I can see though what you see. Do you need glasses to say you have a clean soul?

Money Talks

Are you welcome are is your money welcome?

We feel that if we have money it gives us a pass on how we treat each other.

Then we really see it wasn't US as a people or a person. It was our money. One thing about money its green when it passes from my hand to yours. The color never changes it just fades.

Observations

Are you paying attention? Learn to observe what's in front of you. It can teach you a lot. It's your life

Our Flaws

Once you start a relationship what are you looking for that ideal man or woman?

He opens doors and holds your hand. She cooks your meals and gives you all the sex you desire.

LoL after a couple months things start to differ. You start to execute a plan. You start to see the "flaws" we all got them "Flaws" there's no perfect you or me.

Right Choices

Despair is despair

Anger leads to hate

Hate leads to killing

and other crimes.

Why are we so angry about what's happening to someone else?
Yet ignore our own anger our own hate. We need to find away to help ourselves. Self preservation should come first. Hate does not fix hate.
Ask God to put his arms around you and his hand over your mouth. Choices made in anger cannot be undone.

Struggles or Seasons

Struggles are seasons? Which one are you in now? How many have you been through and how many more will you see? In life there will be struggles within every season. Don't give up.

Solace

Can we find comfort in each other at a time like now? What is the source that we need to help fine peace within our time? Should we be patient with each other as we try to endure this world? No your strength, power and patience.

U.P.S. You

You receive a package it has labels and tags. So why do you let people put you in a box with the same labels and tags? Your package is larger. Therefore you're bigger and outweigh any negative container that most people try and put you in.

US
Me

You

Her

Him

Them

They = US

we are one we can't change who we are.

Can't change the color, age, sex, origin, religion, needs, wants, likes and dislikes. They shouldn't determine US? God doesn't discriminate.

Worry Wart

Why worry what does it fix? "Nothing"

It's really a waste of time. While you're worrying does it change anything? It's only messes with your mind and steals your joy.

After Thoughts

You want people to hear you then pursue you to the highest. Build your platforms and your successes. Then when you look up they will be ready to listen to you. Think of me now see me now. Whatever flowers and rewards you have give them now. When I'm gone I won't see them. The rewards are that I made a difference. May I always be a part of your inspiration?

Acknowledge your feelings and except were you are right now in your life.

About the Author

It's again me at my best standing alone but still standing. One thing about me my loyalty, love, friendships and trust have always been very important in how I live my life. Important in the choices I make and who I share me with. Whatever you do fine a whole based value in how you live, view and allow people to come into your personal space. Whatever I have given you it's genuine. It's ME

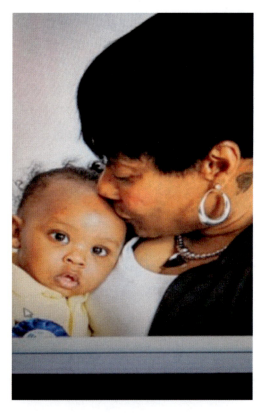

Ace & Me

Made in the USA
Columbia, SC
01 July 2022